I0162497

# CHOSEN ONE

## From Homeless Infant to Priest at Home in my Heavenly Father's Heart

Father Bob Shaldone, SOLT

En Route Books and Media, LLC

St. Louis, MO

# ⊕*ENROUTE*

## *Make the time*

Contact us at contactus@enroutebooksandmedia.com

Cover photo credit: Margie Morin

Copyright © 2021 Fr. Bob Shaldone, SOLT

All rights reserved.

ISBN-13: 978-1-956715-01-9

Library of Congress Control Number: 2021949209

No part of this book may be reproduced, stored in a retrieval system, or transmitted in any form, or by any means, electronic, mechanical, photocopying, or otherwise, without the prior written permission of the author.

# DEDICATION

Dedicated to God the Father, Son, and Holy
Spirit, and to my heavenly mother, Mary,
my spiritual father, St. Joseph, my birth
mother, Geri, my adoptive parents, Helen
and Anthony, and my brother, Paul

# ACKNOWLEDGMENTS

I'd like to acknowledge Dr. Ronda Chervin for encouraging me to write this book and for spending countless hours with me in doing so. I'd like to also thank my publisher, Dr. Sebastian Mahfood, OP, for being willing to publish this book and for spending a number of hours assisting in the proofreading of the text. I'm especially grateful for the endorsements I've received, two of which follow in the next pages. Lastly, for all those who've interceded for this project, in particular the Monastery of the Poor Clares in Boston as well as the Divine Mercy Prayer Ministry in Stockbridge, MA, and for all others who assisted me in other ways in the course of writing this book. A portion of the proceeds from the sale of this book will support the Corpus Christi Hope House, an organization that provides homes for unwed mothers and their children.

# TESTIMONIALS

"Fr. Bob Shaldone's book *Chosen One* is a beautiful depiction of one soul's journey from being an earthly orphan to becoming a chosen son of the Eternal Father. Fr. Bob's life is a great testament to the truth that God makes no mistakes, often writing straight with crooked lines making 'all things work for the good of those who love Him, those who are called according to his purpose.' (Rom 8:28) This book will surely inspire the reader to listen deeper to the voice of God steadily unfolding His plan in their own vocation and life." – Mary Kloska, author of *A Heart Frozen in the Wilderness: Reflections of a Siberian Missionary*

"It is said that St. Pio of Pietrelcina famously opined: '*The earth could sooner exist without the sun than without the Holy Sacrifice of the Mass.*' He might have added that the Holy Sacrifice of the Mass could sooner exist without the earth than without a priest. In Fr. Shaldone's moving autobiography... *Chosen One*... the reader will be treated to a rare, inside look at a marvelous spiritual reality we so often take for granted... the priestly vocation. In addition, as the author relates his life story in a warm, but 'no holds barred' way, the reader will encounter the beautiful mystery of what it means to be human; and in our overly mechanical and often brutally technological society, a development whose dehumanizing effect can be observed all around us, this is no small accomplishment and certainly addresses one of the deepest needs of our times." – Fr. Lawrence Edward Tucker, author of *The Prayer of Jesus Crucified, Adventures In The Father's Joy, To Whom The Heart Decided To Love, The Redemption of San Isidro*

# WHO AM I?

Only when I found my birth mother, Geri Ferrera, when I was twenty-five years old, did I learn about my unusual first months in a hospital in Massachusetts.

In 1952, I was conceived during a date!

My father, Hyman, was an orthodox Jew, son of the lead cantor of a Boston Synagogue, driving a cab in Harvard Square.

My mother was Catholic with a Sicilian background. She was a bookkeeper for a laundry in Boston.

They had been dating for five years. Hyman was in mid-thirties and Geri was in her late-twenties. After a date one evening, he invited my mother up to his apartment. At one point, he began to become intimate with her and surprised her by forcing himself upon her. They were using a condom, which broke.

Obviously, my heavenly father wanted me to be conceived and born into this world. "Oh, happy fault!" as is proclaimed at the Easter Vigil concerning the sin of Adam and Eve that was redeemed by such a death.

Didn't they think about marriage all this time, especially now that Geri was pregnant, I once asked my birth mother?

Hyman was only willing to marry my mother if they would move to Miami because he would be totally shunned by his family if he, an orthodox Jew, married a Catholic.

Geri didn't want to leave Boston.

I found out in the hospital records that my father suffered a depression over this and even wound up in a state facility.

Geri's mother, Lucia, was very upset that her daughter had conceived a child out of wed-lock. One friend suggested she abort me, but she said there was no way she would ever kill a child.

When my mother was about seven months pregnant and began to show, she decided to go to a home for unwed mothers at Tewksbury State Hospital. Because I was slated for a foster-home, she was not allowed to bond with me right after birth.

I was baptized when three days old, June 13, 1953, with the name Keith Anthony Ferrera. It was the feast day of St. Anthony. She chose a first name not ever given in the family. When we were reunited so many decades later, she explained that she didn't want to feel bad every time she was with a relative with my name.

After two months in the maternity ward, I was transferred to a foster-home in Hyde Park. My birth mother visited me from time to time. These foster-parents had several children. According to her, once she found me there in a dark hallway in my bassinet sucking my two middle fingers and smiling at her. She said she smelt alcohol on that woman's breath.

Smiling? Could it be that, by God's grace, I somehow felt bonded to that mother who, in our times, might well have aborted me?

This increased my birthmother's conviction that I needed to be placed for adoption in a better home. She went to Catholic Charities to insist that I be removed from that bad environment. I guessed she could have been ambivalent about whether to try to take care of me herself.

My eventual adoptive grandmother Carmela once told me that when I arrived at the Shaldone house I had rashes, they thought due to not being regularly diaper-changed.

When I was five months old, I was legally adopted by the Shaldone family – Helen and Anthony. The Shaldones were a Church-going Catholic couple. Anthony worked as a heavy equipment operator for the Needham Public Works Department. He had been a boxer in the army during World War II.

Years later, I was told that an injury during World War II led to my father's not being fertile. My adoptive parents were already nine years married before they decided to adopt me and three years later my brother, Paul.

Was it a sign of my being chosen ultimately to become a priest that this adoptive family had chosen the middle name Anthony for me, the same name that my birth mother gave me as a middle name?

What was my childhood like in this new adoptive family? Perhaps, you, the reader, are imagining that now all was well, and I lived happily ever after. Not really?

The good part of being adopted into the Shaldone family was that I was surrounded by extended family. We lived in a large, two family home, owned by my grandparents. My mother's younger brother, Richard, also lived there with his wife, Josephine, and they would have a child soon - Michelle. It happened that I was adopted the day prior to my adoptive mother's birthday. A healing element for my grandmother was that her oldest son, Angelo, a Marine, had died in World

War II at age eighteen on my mother's birth-day. So, in a way, I, having been adopted around a decade later, may have been a con-solation to her. She used to tell me, privately, that I was her favorite grandchild.

The house was in a good neighborhood – working class, but very safe. My dad never even felt it necessary to lock the car doors!

But there were also negatives… psycho-logical reasons why these parents were not able to totally heal the sense of abandonment and not belonging that came with my trau-matic first months of life. This was especially true because my adoptive mother was ex-tremely faithful and diligent but not affec-tionate.

# WHERE DO I BELONG?

Throughout my life I have benefited from much counseling, often professional. As you will see, the root cause of certain patterns was traced back to that first, so unsettled, year of my life.

In summary, psychologists believe that most adults who were adopted out of an orphaned situation exhibit unusually great anxiety.

Counseling began when I was eleven years old. It came about because of this incident. I was playing checkers with my cousin, Michelle, and after I won the game, she was upset that she lost. In revenge, she splurted out that "you and your brother are just a couple of orphans anyhow!"

I was stunned. I knew I was adopted but the word "orphan" was never used by my

Shaldone parents. After all, my birth parents hadn't died.

I ran into the kitchen where my mother and my aunt were sitting. I asked my mother "Are we orphans?"

My aunt lunged out of her chair and ran into the living room and smacked Michelle for being so mean.

Because I was rather withdrawn and seemed very anxious at school, a teacher suggested I could benefit from counseling,

I remember it coming out in counselling that when I was coming home, I would wonder if the house would still be there!

So, somehow the feeling that there was no security for me, no real belonging, showed itself in such ways.

Years later, during a inner healing session in a charismatic prayer group, it came out that I needed to forgive my cousin, Michelle, for trying to shame me by calling me an orphan. I shed tears over this memory.

A sense of insecurity has followed me all my life whenever anyone in some living situation is not friendly towards me.

One form this can take is "fight or flight." If I am in a situation of conflict that I can't seem to resolve, I am torn between my need for the security of stability, but also a desire to find an alternative friendlier living situation.

Fleeing into the Fatherly Heart of God has been my refuge.

# SCHOOL YEARS

When I was about five years old, my mother brought me to meet the Mother Superior of St. Joseph's School in Needham, Massachusetts, staffed by Saint Elizabeth Ann Seton's Sisters of Charity of Halifax, Nova Scotia.

There was a public school across the street. My mother asked me which school I wanted to go to. I remember saying that I chose St. Joseph's, giving the reason I preferred the color of the bricks on their building.

Surprisingly, my mother used to tell people that the very first word I ever spoke was not Mama or Daddy, but God! I pointed to a picture of Jesus that was near my crib when I said this.

In my early years at school, everything was fine. But one of my friends in kindergarten pushed me. I pushed him back. The Sister told me I had to say I was sorry. I didn't want to. But another friend told me that if I didn't apologize, I would have to lay my hand on the steam radiator.

When I was six years old, I came back from a Sunday Mass insisting that I learn trombone. I started with the clarinet and continued with it. By sixth grade, I was selected among others to be a member for the Boston Archdiocesan Youth Symphony Orchestra.

In seventh and eighth grade, some of the wise-guy boys started trying to pick fights with me. One day, I just bashed one of them. My father had coached my brother and me in boxing. To this day, when I feel trampled on, my instinct is to fight back verbally rather than to meekly accept mild persecution. Over time, however, in religious community life, I have learned to forgive more quickly when I feel unjustly treated.

When I finished eighth grade, I went to a Catholic boarding school for ninth and tenth grade. It was a small school with under forty students. I was told years later that this was at the advice of my psychiatrist counselor because of some problem between my mother and myself at home. They seemed to think I was too insecure to transfer to a public school.

My parents visited me every single Sunday and took me out for a hot fudge sundae.

There was Holy Mass every day. I was an altar server. However, unlike some boys who felt a call to the priesthood when serving Mass, I never had that sense of vocation for myself.

Instead, I wanted to be a lawyer or a politician to fight for a better society. It was the time of the assassinations.

I remember just before transferring to the public High School for my junior and senior year, our priest at the small private boarding school told me it would be a great challenge to go from an all boys' private school to a huge public High School.

Amazingly, I did make a good transition. I did well on studies. I played football and ran outdoor track. One thing that helped was that a close cousin of mine, Peter, was in the same homeroom.

Interestingly, I chose to go to Sunday Mass with my grandmother, rather than the Saturday evening Vigil Mass my parents preferred. Carmela, my grandmother, was a strongly devotional Catholic always going to feast-days of Italian saints, and with more statues in her home than we had.

My college years were spent at Boston College with a major in accounting. I lived at home. It was a life-giving time for me. I was in the school's marching band. I dated different girls and assumed I would someday be married since that was the normal path. I wanted to have two sons to fight with each other and a daughter to spoil.

I went to Mass every Sunday. It was the time of liturgical experimentation. I was shocked that Holy Communion was passed around on a plate to be grabbed by the students at Boston College.

During this time, my brother had a huge conversion experience with Born-Again Christians. A few of his friends talked to me. I was trying to get them off my back by telling them I was a baptized, confirmed Catholic. But the Lord seemed to tell me to listen to them.

They led me through 'the four steps': 1) Truly believe that Jesus Christ is the Lord and Savior of the world; 2) Truly believe that every person is a sinner who is destined to go to hell unless he or she accepts Jesus to be their personal Lord and Savior; 3) Truly believe we need a bridge, Jesus, to get from the road to hell to the road to heaven; 4) Truly invite Jesus to be our personal Lord and Savior.

(As Catholics, even though we firmly believe there is a hell, we don't think that someone, for example, who has never even heard of Christ, is going there automatically. Some

theologians even speculate that at the moment of death everyone sees Jesus, and those
who love the good move toward him, but
those who hate the good reject Him.)

They took me through these steps, and I
prayed the "Sinner's Prayer": Lord Jesus
Christ, I am a sinner destined for hell. I do
believe that you are the Savior of the world,
and the only way to avoid going to hell and to
go to heaven, and I am choosing today to accept you as my own personal Savior and the
Lord of my life.

# CAREER AND
# PRIESTLY VOCATION

My first professional job was in June, 1975, working as an internal auditor in the U.S. Navy in Arlington, VA. I was there for a little more than a year and then transferred in August, 1976, to the newly established Navy audit site in Newport, Rhode Island.

I had planned on eventually marrying Diane, the woman I'd been dating for more than a year and a half, and start a family. I thought we would settle down in Newport and "live happily ever after."

One day after Sunday Mass out of the blue, I heard a voice interiorily: "Why not become a priest?"

My thought was "You gotta be kidding!"

I was living with two roommates in Arlington, Virginia. We paid $158 a month including utilities.

During the sacrament of confession, I told a priest "I think I am being tempted to be a priest...but, look, I have a girlfriend I love and a good secure job…"

He responded by suggesting that I could become a married deacon someday.

I thought, "Oh, maybe I can make a deal with God and compromise." But since you had to be thirty-five years old to enter the diaconate program, and I was only twenty-two, this wasn't an immediate choice.

I remember thinking, however, God must know the difference between deacons and priests, so He wouldn't use the word priest if He meant me to be deacon.

But I found myself more and more attracted to the Lord, especially by spending more time reading the Bible.

It was at this time that I got involved with the Charismatic Renewal. Here is how this happened. My brother had given me the famous book by Hal Lindsey called *A New World is Coming.*

If Jesus was really coming back soon, I realized I needed to evaluate my priorities. I decided to talk about this with my parish priest. He suggested I attend a charismatic prayer meeting being held at our parish. It was a mixture of Catholic and Protestant believers.

It did seem strange to me to hear people praying and singing in strange languages. I thought maybe they were crazy. But I also felt a powerful sense of God's presence, peace, and love.

Hearing about the wonderful charitable works the people were doing was also impressive.

At the end of the meeting, the leader invited those who were new to come back at least two more times. "Tonight, you will *think* we are a 'bunch of nuts,' the next time you'll be *convinced* we're a bunch of nuts, and by the third time you'll become a nut as well."

I continued going to this prayer group. After a year's time, someone invited me to go to a famous prayer group in Providence, RI, led by Fr. John Randall. The night before, I happened to see a national news story about Fr. Ralph D'Orio, a popular healing priest. I saw people being "slain in the Spirit" – that is, seeming to faint and lie resting on the floor. I wished I could meet Fr. D'Orio and experience such mystical happenings myself.

In the middle of Fr. Randall's prayer meeting at St. Patrick's Church, Fr. Ralph D'Orio walked in totally unexpectedly.

He announced: "The Holy Spirit told me to get in my car and leave Worchester, MA, and drive here to your prayer meeting. Now, five people here have back problems, and you are being healed."

Sure enough, five men came forward and he told them to bend down and touch their toes. They all could do it. Then he told them to run laps around the gym.

He retired to the back of the hall inviting anyone who wanted to be prayed with to come back there.

I joined the mob of people. I didn't think I could possibly get to him. And then this thought crossed my mind: "If this being slain in the Spirit is real, coming from You, Jesus, I don't need this priest to lay hands on me. You can do it directly."

Instantly, I fell onto the floor. I didn't hurt my head, and the people who stepped on me to get to Fr. D'Orio didn't bother me at all.

Tremendous peace!

When I finally sat up, my attention was drawn to the bookrack, and I saw a book by Fr. McNutt about healing. I bought the book. God seemed to tell me to read it as soon as possible. It was not only about physical healings but also about inner healing of memories.

When I went to my usual prayer meeting, I seized the opportunity to be prayed with for inner healing. During the prayer, I had a memory of my cousin Michelle calling me an orphan. I started to weep. The ministers asked if I was willing to forgive her. I did. One of the women opened Scripture and read out from John 17:1-10 entitled Jesus' High Priestly Prayer.

Then, she told me that Jesus said to me through her: "Be my apostle!"

I immediately related this command to the call I had previously experienced to consider the priesthood!

Trying to take in this huge grace and apply it to my life, I asked one of the prayer leaders about whether the words might mean to be a lay apostle.

One of the leaders suggested I might become a minister in a Protestant Church and then, later, if the Catholic Church allowed for married priests, I could do that.

I knew that I could never leave the Catholic Church.

Later that year, I was baptized in the Holy Spirit. It happened in this way. I was reading Acts 19:1-8 about St. Paul in Ephesus where he asked them if they had received the Holy Spirit. They said they had never even heard of the Holy Spirit.

Two months later, I was back in Boston, and Diane and I decided to make a Life in the Spirit seminar together. When the leaders laid hands on us to receive the gifts, the first thing that happened was that a deep sense came over me of God's being my own personal Father. I also received the gift of tongues and of prophecy.

Some people hearing my tongue at prayer meetings think it is a form of Hebrew. Prophecy is not, as some think, about foretelling the future. As a gift of the Spirit, prophecy is speaking out what one thinks God is telling this group, or one particular person, now. As in "My little children, I am preparing a home for you. I am well pleased with you."

# FINDING MY BIRTH MOTHER

During the Life in the Spirit Seminar, there was a session about inner healing. A Sister Margaret told her story of how she dealt with being an adopted child. She talked about how when she was craving affection, her adoptive mother would just give her an orange!

When the retreat was over, I had an enormous sense of insecurity. Within a day I started thinking that I had to find my birth mother.

I went to the courthouse and requested the adoption records. The judge was reluctant to give me these records thinking I should be grateful for my adoptive parents. A year later, there was a federal law allowing adoptive children to see such records!

Nonetheless, I was able to get those records by searching on my own. I called the place where I was baptized and got my original name: Keith Anthony Ferrera.

I went through all sorts of records at different places and finally was able to track down Geraldine Ferrera in Somerville, MA.

I wrote a nine-page letter with photos of myself from infancy to the present. I was afraid that if I mailed it and didn't get a response, I would never know if she had gotten it or not.

I thought about phoning her, but I was afraid it could give her a heart attack to call out of the blue, telling her, "Hi, I'm your son!"

So, I decided I needed to go to her house and hand-deliver it. My adoptive father came with me at the suggestion of my adoptive mother.

We got there in the middle of the afternoon and rang the doorbell. A woman my age opened the door.

"We're looking for Geraldine Ferrera."

"Let me see if she's upstairs now."

"Geri," she announced. There's a couple of Jehovah's Witnesses downstairs. Should I send them away?"

"No, I'm not afraid. I'll talk to them."

A woman of 5'2" of medium build, dark brown hair, attractive, of middle-age came forward smiling.

She asked, "What can I do for you?"

I extended the envelop with my letter in it.

She opened it right away.

The first thing she pulled out was my baby-picture at 5 months old.

She recognized it and said, "Is one of you guys, Keith?"

I smiled. "It isn't him," pointing to my Dad. "He's older than you. It's me."

"Well, what are we doing standing here? Come upstairs. Have a cup of coffee."

In the kitchen was my demented grand-mother. My mother introduced me to her. "This is my mother, Lillian."

My grandmother responded, "He's not going to knock my teeth out, is he?"

I said, "Not today!"

My mother at that point gave me a big hug with tears running down her face.

Over her head, I saw a picture of the Sacred Heart of Jesus!

In an earlier section of this book, I told you about many things she related to me about her mentality at the time of my conception and about my birth father.

Here, I want only to state that we became good friends. We met monthly and on special holidays. I always spent time first with my adoptive family so they wouldn't feel replaced in my heart.

What about my birth father?

My birth mother told me she believed he was in a nursing home in Cambridge. I found that place. I went into his room. He had light blue eyes, medium height, and a receding greying hairline.

I introduced myself as Bob Shaldone. He didn't know who I was. He showed me the sports' pictures on his wall.

Eventually, he told me he was going to a prayer meeting.

I knew he was Jewish, so I was surprised.

I asked if I could come with him.

He said, "Sure."

During the meeting, there was a break and he finally asked., "How do I know you?"

"Well, do you know Geraldine Ferrera? She is my birthmother, and she told me you were my father."

His eyes widened and he asked, "What do you want from me?"

"I just wanted to meet you. I'm not looking for money or anything. I just want to meet you."

"Well, Geri may have had other men in her life. How do you know it was me?"

The head of the prayer meeting rebuked me for starting an argument.

My birth father, Hyman, walked away fast.

"What are you walking away for?" I asked.

I followed him down the hall. He went around a corner.

Then I heard him laughing at the nursing station.

I thought of confronting him.

Then a man in a wheelchair asked me the time.

God seemed to tell me that it was time for me to leave.

I never saw him again, but I phoned him on Christmas that same year, wondering if he had become Christian.

He was civil and friendly on the phone.

The call lasted about fifteen minutes but neither of us brought up the subject of our relationship.

I called him a year later when Passover and Easter fell at the same time. He thanked me for the greeting.

Whereas the meeting with my birth-mother was healing, the incidents with my father left me cold. My heart was so guarded that I didn't consciously feel hurt.

But the Lord seemed to tell me, interiorily, "See what I saved you from."

In terms of forgiveness, I certainly have tried, trusting that God is healing me from the pain of rejection.

# SELECT PHOTOS

Fr. Shaldone's mother, Helen's,
High School Graduation Picture

Fr. Shaldone's Adoptive Mother and Father
at their Wedding

Fr. Shaldone's Childhood Home
in Needham, Massachusetts

Fr. Shaldone and his Brother Paul

Young Fr. Shaldone and his Clarinet

Fr. Shaldone and his Brother Paul
at Home

Fr. Shaldone's Childhood Home at Christmas (circa 1958)

(From right to left) Fr. Shaldone, Paul,
and Cousins Dickey and Mickey

Fr. Shaldone's First Holy Communion

Fr. Shaldone and his Adoptive Father Anthony at Cushing Hall

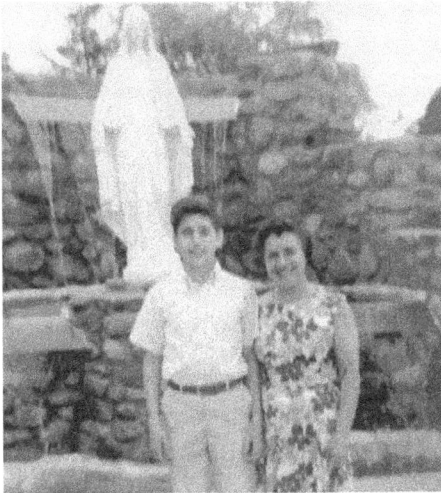

Fr. Shaldone and his Adoptive Mother
Helen at Cushing Hall

Fr. Shaldone's High School Graduation

Fr. Shaldone's Ordination Day
with his Birth Mother

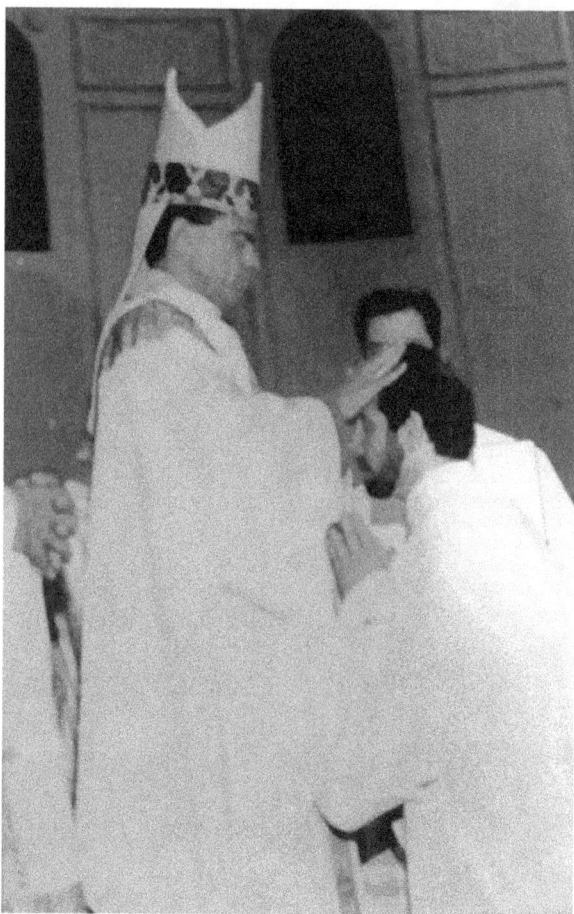

Fr. Shaldone's Ordination with
Bishop Roberto Gonzales

Fr. Shaldone's Ordination Day, after the Ordination

Fr. Shaldone's First Mass at
St. Anthony Parish in Robstown, TX, which
became his first assignment

Fr. Shaldone's Ordination Classmates with
SOLT Founder, Fr. Jim Flanagan, and
Bishop Roberto

# BECOMING A PRIEST

How did Diane, my beloved girlfriend, respond to my vocational call?

I didn't want to tell her that I was leaving her to become a priest. But she had been at the prayer meeting where I got those words. All along, she was aware I was struggling with the thought I might be called to be a priest. At that point, we started dating less often.

I took a leave of absence from my accounting job with Health, Education, and Welfare. I spent a summer with the Oblates of Mary Immaculate trying to discern about this vocation. I didn't feel at that time that I should join that religious community.

When I returned to work, I was getting a sense I needed to leave the accounting world, and to get a job hands on in human services. My new job involved helping mentally challenged adults in my hometown of Needham.

At one point, Diane and I spent a day at Our Lady of Fatima Shrine in Holliston, MA. We spent our time walking outside while praying the rosary.

At the conclusion of the rosary, Diane paused beneath the crucifix and slowly removed the engagement ring from her hand and gave it back to me. "Bob, I really believe that God wants me to set you free to pursue your vocation to the priesthood."

I did not want to take the ring back but finally did with tears. Diane and I are still to this day very good friends.

When telling my story to a friend, she asked me this question: "Could it be that your desire to belong led you to want to totally belong to the greatest man Who ever lived, Jesus Christ, as His brother, friend, bride, and priest?"

"Not necessarily consciously," I responded, but I do see how my strong need to belong was fulfilled in part by this vocation. So often,

God does use our wounds to draw us closer to Him.

I also think that the choice of becoming a priest in a religious community rather than in a diocese was related to the need to belong to a family. So often, the parish priest is alone in his rectory, and the "father figure" – the Bishop – can be transferred at any time.

In the fall of 1980, I applied to the Franciscans. I was accepted into their community in the formation program, which I began in Melrose, MA.

Did I feel I belonged? Yes, in many ways. I loved St. Francis and St. Anthony, my patron saint, and I felt close to the members of the community.

But because of certain major moral problems in the community, I eventually left.

I was so hurt by this experience that I even considered leaving the Church. One Easter morning, I was on my way to a Lutheran Church, but before I turned right to go there, I noticed a statue of Jesus praying in the Garden of Gethsemane. God the Father seemed to tell me distinctly, "Don't leave My Church. I need you to help rebuild and renew My Church."

I took some odd jobs. One of them only lasted a few days because when I had to listen to the other men who were drinking beer and talking about their wives in a nasty way, I decided this is not the place for me.

In January of 1984, I attended Franciscan University of Steubenville to study graduate theology. At the end of the spring semester, I visited a community of Sisters who were trying to form a male branch. When that didn't work out, I went back to Boston.

In the fall of 1984, I decided to join a L'Arche community...a movement founded by Jean Vanier where mentally challenged adults lived with assistants. I did very well with the challenged adults. It was a very life-giving experience, but, overall, it was too active for me. I have always felt called to a more contemplative life.

In the fall of 1985, I entered the Oblates of Mary Immaculate as a postulant with a view to the priesthood. During the pre-novitiate, my adoptive Dad died. I entered the novitiate in the fall of 1986. After six weeks in the novitiate, my novice director suggested I meet with a psychologist to talk about the effect my Dad's death was having on me.

The psychologist affirmed I was in the best place and ought to stay, but my novice director told me to leave. I thought the problem didn't have to do with my psychology; rather, I'd been challenging a priest who was teaching that Jesus didn't physically rise from the dead.

When I returned to Boston, I providentially found within twelve days a place to live with a friend, a job working with special needs people, and a car, all in the midst of a national recession. During this time, I felt God's presence carrying me through. I began going to daily mass and spending time in adoration. It was not hard for me to still sense the call to the priesthood.

In May of 1989, I joined a charismatic covenant community called the Servants of the Cross in Maine. There, I was living with a brotherhood. It was one of my most positive and life-giving experiences.

I had considered marriage while living with the Servants of the Cross, but the call to the religious life and, possibly, the priesthood was still alive in my heart.

One Saturday morning, I was at St. John the Baptist Church in Brunswick, Maine. I was trying to decide if I should reapply to the seminary. I then sensed God the Father ask me once more to look into the priesthood. This would be my third attempt.

I argued with God that there was no way I could go through another failed attempt at the priesthood.

I found myself in the sanctuary standing behind the altar and looking up at a rosetta window above the choir loft. In the stained glass, I saw an image of God the Father.

I said to Him, "Unless you guarantee me the right diocese or the right community, I can't answer Your call."

God seemed to reply: "Do you realize where you are standing?"

It dawned on me that I was actually standing where the priest would be standing during the celebration of the Eucharist while looking up at that window.

"I don't give guarantees because I choose not to control the free will of human beings. Even if the leaders are good, that could sour at any time. But, even without guarantees, will you say 'Yes' to My call to you to be My priest?"

I nearly fell over. I took a deep breath. Finally, I looked up at the picture of the Father in the window and said, "If it really is You, Father, asking me, I will try again. I do want to please You!"

I walked out of the Church to get some air…and God said: "Look straight up. Look at the steeple."

There was an eagle with a fish in its mouth right over the steeple. Following it was a little eagle.

Instantly, I got the message from Jesus, "If you follow Me, I will make you a fisher of men."

It was June 29, 1991, the Solemnity of Sts. Peter and Paul.

# SEMINARY

I was led to Holy Apostles College and Seminary in Cromwell, Connecticut. This is a seminary founded by Fr. Eusebe Menard, OFM, to foster priestly vocations of older men. It was administered by his religious community: Missionaries of the Holy Apostles. Some men came to study at the seminary who were not sure whether they wanted to become diocesan priests or order priests. The hope was that after a year of study they would be better able to discern this aspect of their calling.

My four years at the seminary was joyful, peaceful, and life-giving. We had some of the best professors of philosophy and theology within the United States. The community was made up of some ninety men all the way from men in their twenties to one who was eighty when ordained.

During this time, I met the founder of the Society of Our Lady of the Most Holy Trinity (SOLT), Father James Flanagan. Through my second year, seventeen members of the Society, representing 20% of the student body, were at the seminary.

Once when we were talking amiably, this warm holy priest looked at me and invited me to consider going that summer to help at an orphanage in Mexico that his community served in.

"Bobby, we don't want anything for you except what Our Lady wants."

Even though I bonded well with members of the SOLT community, I still needed time to fully discern that this community was right for me.

A year later, in my second year at the seminary, on Our Blessed Mother's Birthday, September 8th, I asked her if she would guide me to the right community. Please let me know within a week.

Sure enough, exactly one week later, I was sitting at Mass between two SOLT seminarians who were brothers. When I came back from receiving Jesus in the Eucharist, I strongly sensed the presence of our Blessed Mother. She seemed to say: "I know you are leaning elsewhere, but you need a community where you will be able to experience, in the way that suits you best, my motherly love of you. That will help me lead you into a deeper relationship with myself, and the Father, the Son and Holy Spirit. The Society of Our Lady of the Most Holy Trinity will help you the most."

I applied to this community a month later and while waiting for my acceptance, which came within a month, continued to pursue seminary studies.

Only because of the intimacy of Jesus' love for me could I even enter the seminary much less a religious community and embrace the idea of a priestly rather than marital vocation. Once I was in the seminary environment, however, I found that the celibate life was not such a terrible struggle.

People often wonder how young men can even contemplate the idea of celibacy. I say that it was a tremendous challenge for me to even consider the priesthood with celibacy as a requirement. After all, I had had a girlfriend I had been dating for a long time. It was the love relationship that mattered the most to me, but still the physical side also mattered.

Another question people have involves money. In most religious communities, the members have to give any assets they have to the society or give it away before taking final vows. But in the Society of Our Lady of the Most Holy Trinity (SOLT), this was not a requirement because SOLT is a Society of Apostolic Life, and all such societies do not require personal poverty of their members.

So, since I had money from savings when I was working, and also help from my family, finances were not a concern for me, and I was able to pay my way through seminary.

## ORDINATION: A PRIEST AT HOME IN HIS FATHER'S HEART

During the year of seminary, prior to the deacon ordination, we were on retreat and, at one point reference was made to a treatise on the priesthood by St. John Chrysostom. I was reading about how before his ordination, he went through a time when he felt so totally unworthy that he ran away.

I thought, "If this doctor and father of the Church thought he was unworthy, I certainly am unworthy."

Since at this time there was much more publicity about sexual scandals involving priests, I was afraid that I could one day also cause scandal in a moment of weakness.

I was taking a break, shooting pool, and a priest-professor walked in and said, "That's a fine thing, playing pool during a retreat!"

I said, "I just needed a little break, Father," but my real thought was, "I'm out of here!"

Later that day, during a retreat session the thought came that seemed to be from Jesus: "Even if you would fall and create the biggest scandal in the Church, do you believe that I would forgive you?"

I took a deep breath, and I was able to respond, "I do believe."

This gave me confidence to continue on toward ordination because of Jesus' merciful love for me.

I belonged in the Heart of my Father forever.

To my great joy, my birth mother, Geri, came to my diaconate ordination along with my brother, Paul. Both of my adoptive parents had passed away before this time.

Because the ordination occurred at Holy Apostles, the entire seminary community was also present, including all the seminarians who were members of the Society of Our

Lady, and Fr. Jack Purtell, SOLT, who was officially representing the Society.

During the homily, the Bishop told us we needed three virtues to be good priests: the three P's. Look at the tabernacle and see on the wall above the word PRAYER. To the left, the word PERSPECTIVE. And to the right, the word PERSEVERANCE.

These "P's" have stuck with me throughout my whole priesthood of almost twenty-five years.

I had only six months to go before Ordination to the Priesthood. That time in seminary was blessed.

I was so excited, somewhat the way engaged couples are as they prepare for the wedding. Invitations, cards with the date, and the prayer for guests to say for me, etc.

I was ordained to the priesthood with six other members of the Society on June 7, 1997, at the Cathedral in Corpus Christi, Texas.

Because the very name of the city, Corpus Christi, mean the Body of Christ, I felt a deep sense of belonging to the Body of Christ for the purpose of serving the Body of Christ so we can all become the Body of Christ.

My motto on the bottom of the card for my ordination had on it these words that I composed: "Come let us magnify our Lord together forever." Thus, reminding the reader of Our Lady's Magnificat.

Significantly enough, my birth mother and I were able to stay together at a Motel 6 for six days surrounding the Ordination.

When I was placed in my seat in the sanctuary awaiting the ordination, I could see right near me the statues of the Infant Jesus of Prague, St. Joseph, and the Immaculate Heart of Mary. There was a statue of St. Therese nearby, and a stained glass window of Abraham and the sacrifice of Isaac.

These images increased my sense of finally belonging because my birth mother had pinned a medal of the Infant Jesus of Prague on me, which remained with me while I was in the hospital, the foster home, and at my new adoptive home.

St. Joseph was the patron of my home parish in Needham, MA, and I had a strong devotion to the Immaculate Heart of Mary. St. Therese of Lisieux was the first saint I really got to know more personally through reading her autobiography *The Story of a Soul.* And the image of Abraham and Isaac tapped into my Jewish roots.

During the time in the ordination where all the priests to be lie face down on the floor, the litany of the saints is chanted over us. I was hoping to hear the name of my patron saint, St. Anthony. At that moment, I had a deep awareness of my adoptive parents, Anthony and Helen Shaldone, looking at me from above. They were dressed in white with a big smile on their faces.

Two other significant moments for me during the ordination were the anointing of the ordinand's hands with the sacred chrism to consecrate them to the service of God, and the laying on of hands by the Bishop on each of our heads. These two moments are at the very heart of the ordination ritual.

At the conclusion of the ordination, the mothers of the ordinands went up to the altar to greet Archbishop Gonzales. He could see that my mother couldn't get up the stairs, so he got up and walked down to her.

On the way out, I was the last one of the ordinands to leave the sanctuary. When I entered the vestibule, I looked over to the left and found I had a few moments alone with a statue of St. Anthony. I thanked him for helping me arrive at this precious and sacred moment within my life.

My first Holy Mass was at St. Anthony's Church in Robstown, which would be my first assignment. Newly ordained priests are usually quite anxious about doing everything right at their first Mass. Some friends of mine drove all the way from New Mexico, just under a thousand miles away, to be there.

So, even though I was a little nervous, I was also deeply moved to be finally consecrating the bread and wine into the Body and Blood of Christ.

**A Mother's Reflection to Her Son as He Approaches**
**The Greatest Experience of His Life –**
**The Honor of Receiving the Sacrament of Holy Orders**

My son, my boy, my gift from God:
A source of joy straight from the Lord
In the past, we've endured a long separation,
But, now's the time for celebration!

Something told me right from the start
That we would not always be apart
Because the bond between mother and son
Is a mighty strong and lasting one.

Good things come to those who pray,
I prayed that there would be a day
When God would bring you back to me
So that I could witness what I prayed for constantly:

Your Ordination! —blessed from above
Surrounding you with his grace and love
But, now I'm praying that, we won't <u>again</u>
Be apart for a long duration.
It seems to me we've already had a long (and un-
wanted) separation!


God bless and keep you in His Loving Care
Especially since I can't always be there.


Endless love,
Naturally,
Mom

# THE JOY OF BRINGING JESUS TO OTHERS IN THE SACRAMENTS

Once I was ordained, I realized what an awesome privilege it is be an instrument to help others encounter the living Lord Jesus in each of the sacraments of the Church.

For example, in the sacrament of baptism, I have the privilege to initiate a person into the family of the Heavenly Father.

Giving Holy Communion, the Holy Eucharist, to young children for the first time is a delight. Sometimes, I see a twinkle in a young 'eye'. One of my ministries was to the developmentally challenged. I loved to witness their childlike openness and ability to welcome not only other human beings but also the Divine Jesus Himself.

In my second year as a priest, I prepared young adults to come into full communion with the Catholic Church. At the Easter Vigil, I baptized one of them, confirmed seven of them, and administered to all of them their first Holy Communion. I was asked to chant the Exsultat, the story of salvation incapsulated in a long series of joyful exclamations.

Another graced time is preparing couples for the sacrament of marriage. I was touched to be able to be invited into the personal journey of such couples. In particular, when there were couples living together for a long time, one time even seventeen years, some-times married only in civil law, it was wonderful to help them get their marriage blessed by the Church.

Confession! To bring people back into the state of grace through the forgiveness of their sins, especially when they had been away from confession for a long time. Once on Divine Mercy Sunday, I was in the Cathedral of Sts. Peter and Paul in Providence,

Rhode Island. I was ready to leave because no one seemed to be coming, and the lights were being turned off. I went to the men's room. When I came out, I felt the Holy Spirit leading me back to the confessional. I said, "But there's no one coming." The Spirit told me, however, that He was sending someone. Sure enough, a man shuffled his way to the confessional. When he began to speak, he told me he had been away fifty years from the sacrament. He had been a prison guard in one of the worst concentration camps in Europe. And here I am with my Jewish background able to bring the mercy of God to a person who could have been complicit in the death of some of my own family members!

Anointing of the Sick – in my early years as a priest, I was called to anoint an elderly man in a local hospital. I was told by the nurses he didn't have much time left. He wasn't responsive. I went into the room. There were a number of family members watching football. I came to his bed and anointed him with the sacrament of the sick. Shortly afterwards, he sat up in bed and asked what the score of the game was! You should have seen the look on the faces of the family members. Only I seemed to realize that Jesus had practically raised him from the dead!

Another time, I was a full-time hospital chaplain. It was Easter morning. I was going to the hospital to make my rounds. As usual, I proceeded to the intensive care unit. On the way, I wondered how do I greet people close to death with the words "Happy Easter"? God had an Easter gift for me, his priest. In the first room I entered, there was a man I had anointed on Good Friday. His wife had asked for all life support to be removed against my advice and the advice of one of the doctors. She told me, "I've already called my daughter. We're ready to let him go." When I walked in, he was wide awake, totally alert, and said, "I don't know what I'm doing in the hospital. I'm feeling fine." I almost fell over. "I have to get back to my Third Order Dominican lay group to help out."

"Where is your wife?"

"I haven't seen her."

I checked with the staff, and they couldn't find any of the family members in the hospital.

# MY PRAYER LIFE AS A PRIEST

Personal prayer must be the foundation of the life of any priest. I could never survive, never mind grow, as a man and a priest without a deep life of prayer.

My very vocation came when I went from only saying habitual morning and night prayers to growing into a more intimate relationship with God, the Most Holy Trinity.

I want to focus on the absolute necessity of a daily Holy Hour before the most Blessed Sacrament. I heard this first from Archbishop Fulton Sheen, who strongly exhorted priests to make a holy hour every morning.

It has been the lifeblood of my priesthood. It helps me overcome all kinds of discouragement coming from the spiritual warfare we all go through. It gives me the spiritual energy to serve even when fatigued or ill.

In short, my prayer life is among my greatest blessings.

In this context, I am thinking you, the reader, could imagine from what I have written thus far that my life as a priest has been without difficulty because of the way I've managed my prayer life.

Not so!

Looking back, I believe that my wounded psychological background has made my life as a priest and a community member difficult in specific ways. I do not think it would be helpful to spell these out here, but I do realize that others can find me difficult even in ways I don't myself understand. For example, maybe because of my abandonment issues, I try to control the environment around me in ways that others find uncooperative. Nonetheless, I have many good friendships in community.

My relationship with the Holy Spirit, in particular, has enabled me to grow not only in union with God Himself, but also with my brothers and sisters in Christ. It also has equipped me with many spiritual gifts to serve God's people.

Over my two and a half decades of priesthood, one of my prayer ministries has been outside of abortion clinics. I began that way before becoming a priest. With other pro-lifers, we pray the rosary, offer women alternatives, and often give them a free place to stay before and after the birth.

## AM I A JOYFUL PRIEST?

I often tell men who are discerning priesthood, "Don't go in because you are seeking to be happy as in self-fulfillment, but to respond to our Father's invitation to help build His kingdom here on earth!"

Not that there isn't happiness and self-fulfillment in being a priest, but it needs to be the reward rather than the motive.

For me, it all comes down to truly wanting to please my Heavenly Father and to accomplish His will in my life and all the lives I touch.

At one point, my religious superior asked me to go to England to serve in the Society of Our Lady of the Most Holy Trinity mission there. Even though that parish is in a beautiful location in Hythe, which is on the English Channel, I was apprehensive about such a big move. Some psychologists think that people who were given up for adoption by their birth parents are especially fearful about any changes of place.

I agreed to go out of obedience, and I was delighted to find that, when I arrived, I felt deep peace. I never slept better in my life. It came from that total surrender. The key was that I was trying to be pleasing to my Father in heaven instead of just wanting my own way. God's GPS system is better than mine!

In general, in my community, priests are occasionally asked to go to one or another of our international missions. If it is God's will, then I am always blessed despite initial hesitations. There is real peace and joy knowing that I am making my Father happy.

Way back before, when I was discerning priesthood and still engaged to Diane, in prayer God the Father said to me, "I am not calling you to be celibate so you can be more available to be used by Me to do My work, but rather so that you can grow in your relationship with Me." It was as St. Paul explained in

1 Corinthians 7 about how the married man is divided between pleasing his wife and pleasing God, but the single man is called to please God alone.

For the most part, even when enduring heavy crosses in my life as a priest, there is a deep inner joy and peace within my heart. In a way, my Italian cultural background encourages lots of talk about one's crosses. For example, when I was a youngster, if I ever complained about anything, someone in the family would immediately tell why they were suffering as well. So don't be jealous of me, thinking I have l fewer crosses!

On the one hand, as a group, we tend to be more transparent than people of some other backgrounds, wearing our feelings and thoughts on our sleeves. This can be good in many ways, but in the negative, we can overly dramatize our problems and under-emphasize our blessings.

With God's help, I am growing to focus more on the blessings in my life instead of the crosses and challenges I face. I still have a good way to go yet in this area.

# CONCLUSION

My prayer and hope is that what I have shared with you in this booklet will inspire and encourage you to accept Jesus Christ into your heart as your personal Savior and Lord at a deeper level. Then, freely and intentionally decide to fully surrender your entire life – your past failures and successes, your fears and anxieties in the present moment, as well as your dreams and hopes for the future – into Jesus' loving and almighty hands, giving Him full permission to do whatever He sees best in every dimension of your life. Then, to choose to fully cooperate with whatever Jesus decides to do – whatever gifts and graces He blesses you with as well as whatever crosses He sends to challenge you with in order to help form you into His very beloved disciple, friend, and apostle as well as a very beloved child of your Heavenly Father!

Although I have had my share of crosses to bear throughout my life, including some fairly heavy ones, I have come to agree with the late Archbishop Fulton Sheen that "life is worth living"! My prayer for you is that as you prayerfully reflect upon your own life, you will come to the same conclusion. One of my favorite passages from the Holy Bible is from St. Paul's Letter to the Romans, chapter 8: 28: "We know that all things work together for good for those who love God, who are called according to His purpose." (NRSV)

God bless, guide, and keep each of you close to Him throughout your lives!

May you fully accomplish our Heavenly Father's plan for your life and experience the deep peace and joy that comes from co-operating fully with God's will.

May Jesus, Mary, and Joseph carry you into the loving heart of your Heavenly Father where you will be truly at home both now and into eternity!

# TO VIEW AN INTERVIEW
# OF FR. BOB SHALDONE
# BY DR. RONDA CHERVIN –
# GO TO THIS LINK:

https://youtu.be/Jl_US6QlAco

www.ingramcontent.com/pod-product-compliance
Lightning Source LLC
Chambersburg PA
CBHW060137050426
42448CB00010B/2165